# Coyote and Locust

A Zuni story adapted and
Illustrated by Anna-Maria Crum

# Characters

**Coyote**          **Locust**

**Gopher**          **Pigeon**

**Narrator**

**Narrator:** The sky stretches over the **desert** like a shimmering blue flag. Gopher is busily digging burrows and Pigeon is soaring overhead, looking for delicious berries to eat. Coyote is out hunting when he hears Locust singing in a tree.

**Locust (*singing to the tune of "Old MacDonald"*):**
I'm a Locust and I play
Music all day long.
My legs go rubbing back and forth
This is how they sound –
With a click, click here,
And a click, click there,
Here a click, there a click,
Everywhere a click click.
Oh, my music is so slick,
I play all day long.

**Coyote:** What sweet music you make, Locust. Teach it to me.

**Locust:** All right, Coyote. I'll teach you my song. Listen carefully. **(starts singing)**
I'm a Locust and I play
Music all day long.
My legs go rubbing back and forth
This is how they sound –
With a click, click here,
And a click, click there,
Here a click, there a click,
Everywhere a click click.
Oh, my music is so slick,
I play all day long.

**Narrator:** Interested in this development, Pigeon and Gopher stop their activities to listen.

**Gopher:** Locust has a fine voice.

**Pigeon:** A talented performer – he must practise **diligently**.

**Coyote:** That song is so easy. Listen to me sing it. (*singing, badly, to a different tune*) I'm a Coyote and I play…

**Narrator:** Coyote started to sing the song, but he sang the wrong **lyrics**, to the wrong tune.

**Gopher:** That sounds **dreadful**! He makes my teeth hurt.

**Pigeon:** Absolutely **appalling**! He makes my feathers wilt.

**Coyote:** Yeah! My wife will love my song. I must hurry home and sing it to her.

**Narrator:** Coyote scampers away, vigorously singing.

**Pigeon:** He didn't even thank Locust properly for teaching him the lyrics to the song.

**Gopher:** And his howling hurts my ears. I think I'll play a trick on Coyote for making so much noise.

**Coyote** (*singing, to the wrong tune*): I wag my tail back and forth…

**Pigeon:** He memorised the lyrics incorrectly.

**Gopher:** I'm going to keep Coyote from making such a racket.

**Pigeon:** How will you **accomplish** that, Gopher?

**Gopher:** I'm digging a hole in the trail. Coyote is so busy singing, he'll never see it.

**Pigeon:** **Precisely** right. Look, Coyote doesn't see the hole. He's going to fall right into it.

**Coyote:** Ouch! That rotten old gopher made me trip. I've got dirt up my nose and I've forgotten my song. Locust will just have to teach it to me again.

**Narrator:** Dusty and **disgruntled**, Coyote discovers Locust on a rock.

**Coyote:** How lucky you are, Locust. Gopher made me trip and forget the song. You can teach it to me again.

**Gopher:** He acts as if Locust should be thrilled to teach him.

**Pigeon:** You can tell that Locust just *loves* teaching Coyote. What a thankless task.

**Locust (*saying with a sigh*):**
Listen closely this time, Coyote.
(***starts singing***)
I'm a Locust and I play…

**Coyote:** I've got it now.

**Pigeon:** Yes, but for how long, I wonder?

**Narrator:** Coyote jauntily trots away, still without a word of appreciation to Locust.

**Gopher:** There's no way he'll make it back to his home in the canyon without forgetting that song. Then he'll be back to pester poor Locust into teaching him again.

**Coyote (*singing*):**
With a howl, howl here
And a howl, howl there…
(***saying in a proud voice***) How my children will dance when they hear my song!

**Narrator:** Coyote's shrieky song **grates** through the air.

**Gopher:** That sounds even more dreadful than before. And he's *still* singing the wrong words.

**Pigeon:** It's absolutely and utterly more appalling than before.  He screeches the notes so loudly, it's enough to make the rocks crack.

**Coyote (*singing*):**
I'm a Coyote and I howl
In the evening and all day long…

**Gopher:** I can't stand it.  I'm going to bury my head in the dirt.

**Pigeon:** I cannot **tolerate** this racket.

**Narrator:** Pigeon bursts from a bush and flies high up into the air to escape the **cacophonous** noise.

**Coyote:** Silly bird.  You made me forget my song.  Locust will have to teach it to me again.

**Narrator:** Flustered and frustrated, Coyote searches for Locust.

**Coyote (*calling out*):**
Locust, where are you?  You must teach me your song again.

**Narrator:** Fascinated, Gopher and Pigeon watch to see how Locust will react to Coyote this time.

**Gopher:** Locust won't want to teach Coyote his song a third time.

**Pigeon:** I know.  Locust realises Coyote is completely incapable of remembering the song.

**Coyote:** Locust, I'm calling you. I don't have all day.

**Pigeon:** If I were Locust, I'd certainly hide.

**Gopher:** It's time Coyote learned not to be such a pest.

**Locust:** Coyote definitely needs to learn a lesson… but not a singing lesson!

**Pigeon:** What's Locust doing?

**Gopher:** He's **shedding** his skin.

**Locust:** I'll put this rock inside my skin and stick it on the tree. Coyote will think it's me.

**Narrator:** Snickering, Locust hides himself and waits for Coyote to arrive.

**Coyote (*huffing and puffing*):**
Oh, there you are, little friend. Why didn't you answer me?

**Narrator:** Coyote huffs and puffs. He's out of breath from searching for Locust.

**Coyote:** Some silly bird chased the song from my head. You'll have to teach it to me again.

**Pigeon:** He's the silly one. He's so clueless and confused that he doesn't even realise he's not talking to Locust.

**Gopher:** He can't even tell a skin-covered rock from the real Locust.

**Locust:** Coyote thinks the fake Locust is me. I must keep very quiet.

**Coyote:** Hey, Locust. I'm talking to you.

**Narrator:** Coyote sternly shakes his paw at the fake Locust.

**Coyote:** I'll ask you four more times. If you don't start singing your song, I'll crunch you up. Will you sing your song again?

**Locust (*whispers*):** One.

**Coyote:** Sing your song.

**Pigeon (*whispers*):** Two.

**Coyote:** Sing to me!

**Gopher (*whispers*):** Three.

**Coyote:** This is your last chance.

**Locust (*whispers*):** Four.

**Coyote:** All right. You asked for it.

**Narrator:** Coyote leaps forward, attacks, and bites the fake Locust. The rock inside the skin shatters his teeth.

**Coyote:** Ow! Ow! Ow!

**Narrator:** Coyote spits out the rock – and a few **shards** of teeth.

**Locust, Gopher, and Pigeon:** Ha, ha, ha.

**Coyote:** My beautiful teeth are broken.

**Narrator:** Woefully, Coyote shakes his head and slinks home to his family. His tail droops between his legs.

**Locust:** Silly Coyote, I'm glad he's gone. Now I can sing my song in peace. **(starts singing)** I'm a Locust and I play…

**Narrator:** Since that fateful day, Coyote's middle teeth have looked broken…

**Gopher:** …and Locust always sheds his skin.